BRITAIN

IN OLD PHOTOGRAPHS

BLACKHEATH
A SECOND SELECTION

ANTHONY H. PAGE

Sutton Publishing Limited
Phoenix Mill · Thrupp · Stroud
Gloucestershire · GL5 2BU

First published 2002

Title page photograph: The town centre, looking towards Oldbury Road, before the introduction of the ring road. *(CHAS)*

British Library Cataloguing in Publication Data
A catalogue record for this book is available from the British Library.

ISBN 0-7509-2951-0

Typeset in 10.5/13.5 Photina.
Typesetting and origination by
Sutton Publishing Limited.
Printed and bound in England by
J.H. Haynes & Co. Ltd, Sparkford.

A composite postcard of Blackheath, *c.* 1915. *(Ken Rock Collection)*

CONTENTS

THE BLACK COUNTRY SOCIETY

This voluntary society, affiliated to the Civic Trust, was founded in 1967 as a reaction to the trend of the late 1950s and early 1960s to amalgamate everything into large units and in the Midlands to sweep away the area's industrial heritage in the process.

The general aim of the Society is to create interest in the past, present and future of the Black Country, and early on it campaigned for the establishment of an industrial museum. In 1975 the Black Country Living Museum was started by Dudley Borough Council on 26 acres of totally derelict land adjoining the grounds of Dudley Castle. This has developed into an award-winning museum which attracts over 250,000 visitors annually.

In 1998 the Museum Board secured a lottery grant of nearly £3 million towards the £4.5 million cost of building a state-of-the-art interpretation centre. Known as the Rolfe Street Baths Project as it incorporated that Smethwick building which was transferred to the museum site, it was officially opened on 18 May 2001. It includes two fine exhibition halls, administration and storage rooms and retains the original Victorian building's façade. The museum's already wide range of attractions is likely soon to be increased in the field of transport with the acquisition of two major collections of vehicles.

At the Black Country Living Museum there is a boat dock fully equipped to restore narrowboats of wood and iron and different vessels can be seen on the dock throughout the year. From behind the Bottle and Glass Inn visitors can travel on a canal boat into Dudley Canal Tunnel, a memorable journey to see spectacular limestone caverns and the fascinating Castle Mill Basin.

There are 2,650 members of the Black Country Society and all receive the quarterly magazine *The Blackcountryman*, of which 136 issues have been published since its founding in 1967. In the whole collection there are some 2,000 authoritative articles on all aspects of the Black Country by historians, teachers, researchers, students, subject experts and ordinary folk with an extraordinary story to tell. The whole constitutes a unique resource about the area and is a mine of information for students and researchers who frequently refer to it. Many schools and libraries are subscribers. Over 3,300 copies of the magazine are printed each quarter. It is non-commercial, and contributors do not receive payment for their articles.

PO Box 71 · Kingswinford · West Midlands DY6 9YN

INTRODUCTION

'Blackheath – where is Blackheath?' To many people who have no direct connection with the town that is a common response. If, when using modern computer technology to plan routes, the name is entered as starting point, you are often presented with choices, Blackheath, Colchester; Blackheath, Guildford or Blackheath, London; frequently 'our' Blackheath does not deserve a mention. To some extent, it has always been so – even among Black Country folk. When compiling his books on the area F.W. Hackwood, the noted historian, simply writes off the town as 'being of little significance'. Perhaps that had been true when, as the derivation of the name suggests, it was little more than a collection of isolated buildings in a bleak heathland. From ancient maps it appears that the surrounding area consisted of a few run-down farms, with one or two roads passing through, connecting neighbouring towns which were much more important. The glebe land belonged, in the main, to the Earls of Dudley, and it was not until this was released for development that the settlement began to grow, both in size and importance.

White's Directory of 1851 states that 'Blackheath, and some other parts of the [Rowley Regis] parish have greatly increased their population and buildings during the last few years'. Another contemporary directory has the following entry:

Black Heath (or Bleak Heath) is a town and was formed into an ecclesiastical parish on July 13, 1869 out of part of the civil parishes of the Hill & Cakemore, Worcestershire, two of the seven townships attached to the old borough of Halesowen; each of these parishes now has its own parish council, so that Black Heath is partly within the district of the Rowley Regis urban district council and partly within the areas of the Hill and Cakemore parish councils. It is about a mile from Rowley Regis station on the Great Western railway, 3 south-east from Dudley, and 8 west from Birmingham, in the Kingswinford division of the county, Rowley Regis petty sessional division, Dudley union and county court district, rural deanery of Dudley and arch-deaconry and diocese of Worcester.

As was described in *Blackheath in Old Photographs* (Sutton, 2000), the town is right on the border between Staffordshire (Rowley Regis) and Worcestershire (Halesowen), and although the name disappeared from post office recognised areas during the latter part of the previous century, to anyone with a longer memory Blackheath near Birmingham covered the postal district from Rowley to The Stag, Coombs Wood to Whiteheath, and it is this area which has been taken for the contents of this volume. No doubt there will be some who will argue that there are items included which should not have been; equally others will want to know why parts have been omitted.

Blackheath achieved the status of 'boom-town' once the expansion had commenced, and in a later article F.W. Hackwood wrote: 'Blackheath, the daughter, has far outstripped Rowley, the parent.' Indeed, if a comparison were to be made, Blackheath took on the appearance of a commercial centre, with a long High Street, crammed with shops and other business enterprises, while Rowley retained the air of a village.

The centre of Blackheath consisted of the Royal Oak public house, a coaching inn owned by the Darby family, and almost adjacent had been a saw mill, right on the edge of the heath. With an eye to the expanding possibilities William Connop built a large house and draper's shop on the site of the mill in 1865, the place becoming known as Connop's Corner, now the junction of Halesowen Street and the Market Place. The next major development took place in 1937, when to allow for the rapid expansion of vehicular transport the Royal Oak and its outbuildings gave way to the traffic island, still at times a bottle-neck despite the partial introduction of the ring road.

Another glance at trade directories yields an impressive list of names of families connected with the development of the town, names such as Gaunt, Hackett, Sturman, Parkes and Darby, many of whose descendants are still the backbone of the town today. A great many of these people have readily opened their family albums to share the pictures included in this book, and it is amazing what a store of nostalgia is still available. There are, inevitably, things that are missing, and the search goes on. Who, for example, remembers the British Restaurant in Birmingham Road, or a little further up the Civil Defence headquarters, the police stations and their occupants in Holly Road or Nimmings Road, or any of the smaller industrial concerns of the locality? Maybe you have some pictures. If so, I would be pleased to hear from you, and to include them in future works.

One of the direct consequences of the publication of the first volume of old photographs has been the tremendous interest generated in looking at the history and folklore of our town, and an amazing number of people have joined together to form the Blackheath and Rowley Local History Group, which meets monthly, has visiting speakers and pools information for posterity. To find out more details of this, you are invited to contact Blackheath Library in Carnegie Road. Finally, to return to the computer age, the author would like to recommend anyone with access to the internet to turn to a new website set up by a young man named Matthew Johnson, where current, and historical, information is displayed. The address is **www.rowleyregis.com**. So, where is Blackheath? I hope that the reader will find some of it in these pages or on the net, but most of all it lives in the hearts and minds of those of us fortunate enough to have associations with 'this insignificant place'.

Anthony Page, 2002

1
Around & About

The junction of Birmingham Road and Oldbury Road, with the Handel Hotel just visible, is to the rear of the Tilling-Stevens motor bus, parked at what was called the bus terminus, outside the barber's shop belonging to J. Taylor, pictured wearing his white apron. The conductor is leaning on the mudguard of the bus, waiting to take passengers to Quinton. Although the surroundings and the style of transport may have changed through the years since this picture was taken in about 1920, buses still depart to Birmingham from roughly the same spot.
(Roy Parsons)

At the beginning of the last century there was a farm situated in Beeches Road, between the Baptist chapel and the Infant School, and this old postcard is a view of the farmhouse. On the reverse, which is dated 1904, Edith writes to Miss B. Mucklow of 99 Oldbury Road: 'Hope you will like this, it is a portrait of our house with papa outside the door. Do not show it to anyone, as papa being light complexioned is not taken very well.' It is hoped that, with the passage of time, that restriction has lapsed! *(Horace Taylor)*

Joining Powke Lane to Waterfall Lane is Terrace Street, and this view shows the steep incline, and the way the houses were constructed to take account of the slope. Shortly after this photograph was taken, at the end of the 1960s, these houses were demolished to make way for the modern housing development that has replaced them. *(Author's Collection)*

J.W. Willetts's electrical store is empty, and the fly posters have been busy, as Birmingham Road prepares to be redeveloped in the mid-1970s. The Handel Hotel at the junction with Oldbury Road is still open for business, as is the Mother & Baby shop, but as can be seen from the road sign Oldbury Road has already been closed to traffic, with a diversion in operation via the island and Park Street. *(Ron Wood)*

This view was taken from the bedroom window of 58 Uplands Avenue in 1949. It is recalled that whenever the 'nit nurse' visited the street she would park her bicycle by the hedge and telegraph pole, and then proceed to the house in which she was due to work, so as to maintain discretion and not cause undue embarrassment to the family concerned. *(Graham Beasley)*

A postcard view of Waterfall Lane, looking up towards Beeches Road, with one of the many horse and cart deliveries taking place, *c.* 1920. The top part of the thoroughfare does not indicate the steep nature of the road, for many years prohibited to heavy goods vehicles, and even to bicycles! Many of the more wealthy families of the town had houses in the street, including the Lench family who occupied the large property named The Beeches, and the Willetts family, owners of the sweet-making business. Despite the rather pretty sign on the present public house named The Waterfall a little lower down the hill, no-one seems to be able to remember an actual waterfall, common consent seeming to indicate that an overflowing culvert which gave rise to the name of the lane. *(Margaret Adams)*

A view down Blackheath High Street, looking towards the Market Place, *c.* 1940. The market hall can be seen in the distance, and apart from the façade of F.W. Woolworth having moved back a little, the other shops on the left-hand side remain very much the same today. *(Ken Rock Collection)*

This row of old cottages, seen here in about 1970, was in Park Street, opposite the Salvation Army Citadel, until the land was earmarked for development and they were demolished. The drive to the Coronation Social Club is situated at the extreme left of the picture. *(Ray Parkes)*

A dwelling of unusual construction, with the sloping roof covering what today we would call a patio, stood for many years on the corner of Beeches Road (when it was called Tump Road) and Halesowen Street, on the opposite corner to the Beech Tree public house. *(Horace Taylor)*

Almost at the top of Gorsty Hill were these old cottages, with a Mr Harris living at no. 23. The ones in the foreground are still there, extensively modernised, while those at the rear have been demolished and replaced by more modern semi-detached dwellings. At the time of this picture, *c.* 1910, there were no piped utilities, and its owner remembers the excitement when the gas and water mains were laid. *(Elsie Scarrott)*

These old cottages in Ross, opposite the Junior School, were demolished shortly after this picture was taken in 1981, and made way for an improved access to the yard at the rear of John Tooth's builders' merchants in High Street. The fancy terracotta work above the doors and windows was saved and is now in the Black Country Living Museum, Dudley. *(John Tooth)*

This picture, taken in the 1980s from The Causeway, shows the rear of the old Blackheath Electric Pavilion Cinema (referred to by locals as 'The Snob'), which was later used for a variety of purposes (*see* p. 90), with the projection room still in evidence. Originally commissioned by Mr Cooper, it was later sold by him when he built what he referred to as 'The Super Cinema' – the Kings Theatre in Long Lane. *(BCLM)*

A postcard view of the junction of Halesowen Street and High Street, *c.* 1920. To the extreme left of the picture the lamps indicate the position of the California public house. The ladder is against the general hardware dealer of Hobbs, although the well-known sign-writing is not yet in place. *(Ken Rock Collection)*

Heath Street, formerly called Hackett Street, during the heavy snowfall in the winter of 1947. One or two of the householders have cleared their frontages, but the going remains difficult for the valiant milkman making his deliveries. *(Brian Bubb)*

The central portion of High Street, from almost opposite the post office, clearly showing the tram lines that linked Blackheath with Old Hill, 1920s. The last trams operated towards the end of the 1920s, and although originally intended to continue into Oldbury, the extension was never completed because of financial and local authority boundary problems. *(Ken Rock Collection)*

Before it became so congested with traffic Long Lane was still the main connection between Blackheath and the top of Mucklow Hill, but there is an almost rural aspect of this shot, *c.* 1900, which now has a long-lost air of tranquillity about it. The only vehicle shown is the bicycle being wheeled by its owner as he passes a group of workmen engaged in road repairs. This portion of the road is in the general vicinity of the library. *(Ernest Honeysett)*

A 1930s view of Springfield Road from the junction with Woodland Road, before the houses were built on the left-hand side of the road in the 1940s. The farm buildings, where Olive Hill School was later built, are visible at the top of the picture, where the road bears right into Cocksheds Lane. The large house on the extreme right of the picture later became, and still remains, the manse occupied by the Methodist minister of the Blackheath Circuit. *(Frances Dolphin)*

Two more views of the upper stretch of Long Lane at the start of the twentieth century. The top picture has the local children out in force, and is looking towards Blackheath, taken from the opposite side of the road from Long Lane Methodist Chapel. *(BCLM)* The picture below looks in the opposite direction, from a little lower down, with the original Wagon & Horses public house just visible in the centre of the terraced houses on the left-hand side. It is thought that the track leading off to the right eventually became Edward Road. *(Ernest Honeysett)*

The fairly quiet residential area of Beaumont Road, on the opposite side of Masters Lane from Holt Road, 1920s. *(Frances Dolphin)*

Belgrave Road, looking up to Beaumont Road, from the junction with Long Lane at Shell Corner, *c.* 1920. *(Frances Dolphin)*

Just above the junction of Long Lane and Feldon Lane were the Odeon Cinema and Odeon Buildings. The cinema was part of the chain of Odeon Theatres Limited, the chairman of the company being Oscar Deutsch, and was officially opened on 20 October 1934, having been constructed by the local firm of Housing Limited. At the time there were eighteen Odeons nationwide, this being the only one in the Midlands, with another eleven under construction. To the rear was parking space for 250 cars, and the projectors were supplied by British-Thomson-Houston. For many years it was a popular venue for entertainment, especially for the Saturday morning children's performances. *(Harry Brettle)*

With the general decline in cinema-going the Odeon followed the popular trend and became a ten-pin bowling alley (as did its sister Odeon at Warley), before that too lost its appeal. In this picture, taken on 28 April 1974, we see it in its next incarnation, as Tiffany's Dance Hall. However, in time that also closed and for a period the building was turned into the do-it-yourself store of B&Q, but a few years ago that business was moved to the large superstore in Mucklow Hill. At the time of writing (July 2002) there are no occupants, and it is sad to see the magnificent structure boarded up and unused. *(Halesowen Library)*

This aerial view, taken in 1920, shows the area behind Blackheath Market. Oldbury Road is on the left, with the Globe Works in the centre. Travellers' caravans are seen on their designated site, which is situated roughly where the Coronation Club currently stands in Park Street. The cottages behind them are the ones shown on p. 11. Blackheath's first picture house (Blackheath Picture Palace) is towards the top right of the picture in Cardale Street. *(Clarence Siviter)*

On the left-hand side of Holly Road, when facing towards Ross, stood Ivy Cottage (presumably named for obvious reasons), and these other houses, which are seen here in 1932, before being demolished in the 1970s to make way for a redevelopment scheme that has never taken place. *(Ann Green)*

Above: This was the first house to be built in Highfield Road (it is now numbered 34), on the corner of Marlow Street. When Ben Hobbs built it in 1898 it cost the magnificent sum of £200, a considerable amount in those days. Mrs Hannah Tromans is pictured with her mother. *(J. Price)*

The war memorial erected to honour the men of Rowley Regis who fell in the First World War, was placed on the spare land at the bottom of Powke Lane, before the ground was designated as the municipal cemetery. At the time of the photograph, believed to be the early 1920s, there are still miners' cottages and industry occupying the area. *(Martin Pearson)*

Nos 58–60 Halesowen Street awaiting demolition, June 1974. The once carefully tended rear gardens have understandably been allowed to run wild, although the owner of one cottage is attempting to keep the weeds down. This picture was taken just before the houses were demolished. *(Halesowen Library)*

Halesowen Street, looking back towards Blackheath town centre, 1972. Behind the white house on the right-hand side the roof of the Working Men's Club can be seen. The spare ground at the right indicates that redevelopment has commenced, and the houses on the left will shortly make way too for new properties. *(CHAS)*

Ashley Street, Blackheath, with Long Lane in the foreground, led up to the haulage yard of Adam Jones. In this picture, taken in 1969, we see the Ashley Hotel on the right, the Travellers Rest public house on the left, and E&H Filter Co. Ltd in the centre. This comparatively narrow track was soon to become engulfed as part of the Blackheath ring road, and now leads to one of the main entrances to the large Sainsbury's supermarket. The Ashley has been retained, but the industrial premises have turned into Changes Night Club. The cottages and Travellers Rest have disappeared. *(CHAS)*

The vicarage of St. Paul's Church, situated in Vicarage Road, in the early 1960s, before it was replaced with a more modern building. *(Author's Collection)*

A watercolour impression of Cakemore Mansion, which was also known as Cakemore House and Cakemore Farm, and was located on the corner of Masters Lane and Nimmings Road. For a time it was the home of Thomas Adams, whose daughter Ann married Matthias Attwood in 1775 at St Giles's Church, Rowley Regis. They raised ten children, the third of whom, Thomas Attwood, gained fame as the Member of Parliament for Birmingham, and was a noted champion in securing rights for the working man. *(Horace Wilson)*

A view of the Shell Corner area from the air, in the 1950s. The traffic island is visible in the right foreground, with Nimmings Road running off to the right. Long Lane goes vertically, with a bus passing the Congregational church at the top. Shell Corner Buildings stand at the junction with Malt Mill Lane at the left centre, and the developing industrial estate in Victoria Road can be seen at the extreme left. *(BCLM)*

Nimmings Road, formerly Station Lane, looking in the direction of Shell Corner. The old cottages at the left are shown on the Ordnance Survey map of 1883 as the only buildings between Upper and Lower Holt Farms and Cakemore Farm. The terraced housing, which is still standing, was added at a later date. *(David Westwood)*

A postcard view of Fairfield Road, from opposite one of the entrances to the BTH factory, *c.* 1930. Although today the road has been given a coat of tarmac, the houses remain almost identical. *(Author's collection)*

A general view of the upside railcar discharge sidings and boiler house, just outside the station, as seen from the top of one of the LPG storage tanks, 10 November 1966. The houses in Boundary Avenue are at the extreme left of the picture. *(David Parsons)*

A local train enters Rowley Regis station from the Old Hill direction, 1969. At that time the offices of Belgrave (Blackheath) Engineering were situated in Avenue Road, and the outline of St Paul's Church can be seen on the skyline. The structure crossing the railway line is a ducted water supply, and was used for many years by children as a popular (but highly dangerous and illegal) short cut from Avenue Road to Nimmings Road. *(CHAS)*

The entrance to the railway tunnel viewed from the embankment, April 1977. Completed in 1867, the tunnel, which is 896 yards long, enabled the Stourbridge Extension Railway to go from Old Hill to Galton Junction, Smethwick, thus allowing travel between Worcester and Birmingham, and access to the whole railway network. Much labour was imported to undertake the necessary work, and the charm of the visitors is said to have influenced the birth-rate of the local population! The offices of Blackheath Building Society (now Britannia) are on the right of the picture, and the row of shops, including S. Detheridge & Son (drapers) and the Travellers Rest public house, on Long Lane is to its left. *(CHAS)*

The Market Place, looking towards Long Lane, 1958. Although the pedestrian subway was in operation at the time, with the entrance railings at the left of the picture, it was never popular, and as the two ladies shown here testify, people preferred to risk the increasing traffic levels rather than the unknown risk of going below ground. *(Stan Tromans)*

Behind and adjacent to 19 Long Lane were these old stables, seen here in June 1974. *(Halesowen Library)*

The road from New John Street to Upper Ashley Street, seen here in 1974, is now the entrance to a large housing complex. For many years the shop on the corner was a popular retailer. As well as leading to small businesses the road was the entrance to a recreation ground, used by Lenches football team and other sporting activities. *(Halesowen Library)*

Before the road-widening in the days when Narrow Lane lived up to its name, *c.* 1974. We are looking down towards the junction with Feldon Lane and Dale Road, with Newlands Drive going off to the left. The cemetery, operated by Birmingham City Council, is situated behind the trees to the right of the photograph. *(Halesowen Library)*

Beaumont Road, with Belmont Warehouse on the right, 1920. The business sold drapery and clothing, with suits, overcoats, costumes and coats being advertised as ready made or made to measure, at prices which saved the customer 2*s* in the pound. The Warehouse had a large and comprehensive stock. *(Frances Dolphin)*

The bus (seen on p. 7) is now on its return journey from Quinton, coming down Long Lane, almost at the junction with Feldon Lane (on the left). The external appearance of the row of terraced housing on the right of the picture remains largely unchanged today, although most have been modernised internally. *(Maisie Hayman)*

Great Western Railway engine no. 3819 gets up a head of steam as it enters the tunnel from the Old Hill end heading for Blackheath, pulling tanker freight, August 1962. The A frame supporting the tunnel entrance was removed shortly after this picture was taken and the whole structure was strengthened with reinforced concrete. A solitary person is seen watching the event from behind the fence in Highfields. *(CHAS)*

The changing face of the town centre can be seen in these two pictures. The photograph above dates from about 1950 and the large Burton's building is still in a fairly new condition, with its gleaming white façade. The Royal Oak public house and the Shambles were demolished in about 1930 to make way for the traffic island and the new shops. The foundation stones for the Burton's Buildings were laid by members of the Burton family in August 1939. On the middle floor was the Snooker Hall, frequented by many local sportsmen. This was where Rex Williams, later to become World Champion and head of the World Professional Billiards and Snooker Association, first came to prominence. *(Author's Collection)* In the lower picture, taken some twenty years later, the ill-fated building scheme known as the Highshore Development can be seen rising behind The Shoulder of Mutton public house. Originally intended to span Birmingham Road, and bring Blackheath into the modern shopping age, it was blighted by a series of financial disasters. The scheme was never actually opened and finally abandoned, the site eventually becoming Barclays Bank and adjacent car park. *(CHAS)*

2
Schooldays

To celebrate the coronation of HM Queen Elizabeth II in 1953, the children and staff of Powke Lane School re-enacted the ceremony in the school playground. *(Joyce Hodgetts)*

Hill & Cakemore Secondary Modern Boys School, Class II, 1958/9. Back row, left to right: John Gibson, Rex Wheeler, David Johnson, John Kemp, Raymond Nicklin, Lloyd Grainger, David Wootton, Roy Faulkner, David Galley, Stanley Morgan, Graham Hutchinson. Middle row: Ronald Riley, Michael Shakespeare, Paul Hackett, David Harold, Robert Parker, David Munslow, John Smith, Royston Hingley, Peter Hughes, Stephen Rogers. Front row: Michael Lee, Michael Walker, Edward James, Trevor Rose, Michael Pearson, Mr I. Adams (Form Teacher), Trevor Salter, Geoffrey Whitehouse, Alan Bateman, Gerald Taylor, Michael Brawn. Seated: Robert Walter, Peter Bowater. *(John Kemp)*

A group of pupils from Powke Lane School admire the mayoral chain of office, as Councillor George Smith, the Mayor of Sandwell, pays a visit to the school during his year of office, 1980. *(Denise MacDonald)*

Above: Brian Bubb with his classmates outside the woodwork room at Britannia Road School, 1947. *(Brian Bubb)*

Barry Nock, a pupil at Britannia Road Boys School, became schoolboy champion boxer of Great Britain in 1952 in the intermediate class, weighing in at 6 stone 9 pounds. *(Jeff Ostermeyer)*

Class 3A, Beeches Road Junior Mixed School, 1938. Back row, left to right: Cyril Robinson, J. Thomas, Arthur Pearson, -?-, Max Taylor, Ron Wood, John Comley, Ray Bagnall, -?-, Harry Harper. Fourth row: Mr Parkes (head), -?-, Nancy Young, -?-, -?-, -?-, Mavis Mole, -?-, Betty Lashford, -?-, -?-, Iris Andrews, Mr Richards. Third row: Connie Eley, -?-, Betty Green, -?-, Nellie Payne, Hilary Hadley, Alice Winall, -?-, -?-, -?-, -?-, Isobel Hackett. Second row: -?-, -?-, -?-, Iris Eley, Eva Tromans, -?-, -?-. Front row: -?-, Ernie Tromans, Len Turner, Clifford Baker, Geoff Taylor, Horace Adams, -?-, Joe Breakwell, Reg Wallace. *(Nellie Holloway)*

Some members of the Swimming Club at Britannia Road Boys School, 28 May 1960. The school was proud of its swimming and life saving groups, as it had become one of the first schools in the region to have its own swimming pool on school grounds. *(County Express)*

A charming group of girls from Powke Lane School, 1916. Among them is Ethel Taylor. *(Ann Green)*

The Mayor of Rowley Regis, Alderman Reginald Downing JP, presents the Hobbs Cup, which is about to be draped with the colours of Saxons, the winning house by the House Captain, Colin Smith, and the House Master, Will Brittain. This photograph was taken at the Annual Speech Day, 17 July 1958, at Britannia Road School. *(County Express)*

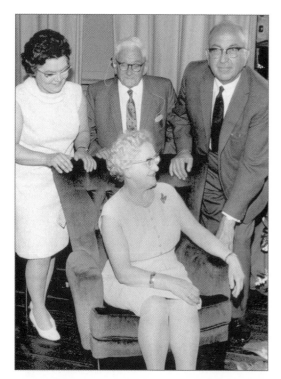

A picture from the *County Express* showing the retirement of Miss E.M. Lyons, who had been Headmistress of Hill & Cakemore Secondary School for Girls from 1942 to 1969. She was presented with many gifts from well-wishers, including two fireside chairs, one of which she is seen testing out. There was a full assembly of the school to mark the occasion, which was presided over by Luther Jones (Chairman of the Governors). *(Halesowen Library)*

Miss Elsie Perry joined the staff of Powke Lane Infant School in April 1934 as an assistant teacher, and remained there, eventually achieving the position of Deputy-Head Teacher, until her retirement in July 1972. She is seen here with her colleagues, including the Head Teacher, Miss Amy Ryder (on the right), at her retirement party. *(Ann Taylor)*

Frank Bolton, seen here on the Britannia Road playing field, achieved international honours when he played football for the England Schoolboys Team. He was capped in 1952 and in that year he played against Scotland, Ireland and Wales, as well as captaining a Staffordshire County XI against a select London squad. At one stage he was in the same team as the late Duncan Edwards. He went on to play professionally for several teams. *(Jeff Ostermeyer)*

Below: The post-war years saw what was called a 'baby boom', which was reflected in many more children needing schooling. The premises at Beeches Road School were not large enough to accommodate all the pupils, and as a result overspill classes had to be held at Birmingham Road Methodist Schoolroom. This is a class of 1954 on the steps of the Sunday School building. It includes Carolyn Cockin, Joan Gardner and Marilyn Davies. *(Jean Ward)*

Pupils and teachers from Siviter's Lane School are pictured on their way, crocodile fashion, down Britannia Road en route to Blackheath station to take part in their annual outing in 1951. This year they were to visit London and Windsor, including a boat trip on the River Thames. *(Maud Shaw)*

Another school trip, but on this occasion the boys from Britannia Road School are on the school steps all ready to spend Easter in Paris. The day of departure was 9 April 1955, and they returned on 17 April. Regulation mackintoshes and suitcases appear to be the order of the day! *(Jeff Ostermeyer)*

Above: A much earlier class at Beeches Road School, *c.* 1910. The only known person is Mercy Willetts, who is second from the left on the front row. *(Dorothy Parkes)*

The Annual Prize Distribution at Rowley Regis Secondary Boys School (Britannia Road), 17 July 1958. Alderman J.P. Pennington, JP, (Chairman of the Governors) and Mr. F.E. Sidaway, (Deputy Head), are seen with the lectern Bible which had been presented to the school by Mr and Mrs. J. Foord in memory of their son, John Spencer Foord, a former school prefect, who had been killed in a road accident in April 1957. *(County Express)*

Blackheath Junior School, Powke Lane, celebrated its centenary on 31 October 1979, and a group of pupils, dressed in mock-Victorian style, are seen celebrating the event during playtime. *(Denise Macdonald)*

A group of school prefects at Britannia Road Boys School, 1959. Back row, left to right: K. Darby, R. Dunn, K. Mellor, J. Horton, C. Priest, G. Harris. Front row: B. Barnsley, A. Bayliss, S. McBride, Mr G.A. Willetts (Headmaster), L. Calloway, E. Winwood, R. Tromans. *(Jeff Ostermeyer)*

A class of boys at the Church of England School in Long Lane, in the early part of the twentieth century. Among the pupils is John Pennington, later to become a Freeman of the Borough of Rowley Regis. *(Kathleen Brain)*

Britannia Road School has always maintained a high record of sporting prowess, and on 28 April 1952 three of the then school champions were entertained by the Mayor and Deputy Mayor of Rowley Regis to mark their achievements. Left to right: Alderman A. H. Hancock JP (Mayor), Barry Nock (boxing), Frank Bolton (football), Kenneth Hackeson (billiards), Alderman T. Deeley JP (Deputy Mayor). *(Jeff Ostermeyer)*

Powke Lane Infant and Junior School orchestra, 1938 or 1939. *(Margaret Guest)*

Local schoolchildren taking the cycling proficiency tests in the playground of Britannia Road School, with the houses of Ruskin Avenue in the background, September 1963. Councillor William Thomas Salt is shown on the left, scrutinising the entrants, with a representative of the local police force in attendance. *(County Express)*

Class 12 of Hill & Cakemore Secondary Modern Boys School, 1958/9. Back row, left to right: Paul Tibbetts, Alan Horton, Robert Woodhall, John Tibbetts, Graham Lowe. Middle row: Bruce Innes, Clive Harvey, Robert Cutler, Geoffrey Loveridge, Robert Watson, William Byng, Raymond Feeney, Richard Dunn. Front row: David Hassall, Raymond Wheeler, Michael Hanney, Kenneth Cole, Terence Palmer, Mr P. Coleman (Form Teacher), Roger Greaves, Paul Allen, Allan Masters, Anthony Hadley, Paul Browning. *(David Hassall)*

The pupils and teacher of Form IIB of Beeches Road Junior School, *c.* 1930. *(Harold Barnsley)*

Blackheath County Infants School, celebrating a harvest festival with a difference. Every child in the school brought along gifts, which were then parcelled up and delivered to elderly relatives or children who were sick. Over 200 such packages were distributed after the service. The headmistress, Miss A.V. Ryder, is seen with some of the pupils getting the parcels together. *(Freda Smith)*

A group of boys look on enthusiastically at the School Sports Day at Rowley Regis Secondary School for Boys (Britannia Road), 1953. Among those identified are Colin Bagley, Jim Sidaway and Wesley Potter. *(County Express)*

3

Work & Leisure

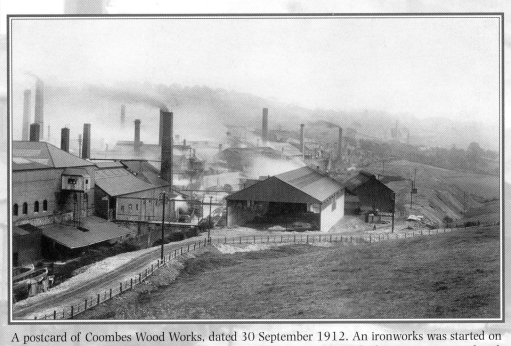

A postcard of Coombes Wood Works, dated 30 September 1912. An ironworks was started on the site in 1860, making tubes for water, steam and gas. In 1870 the business was joined with that of Lloyd & Lloyd, who in turn joined with Stewarts & Menzies to become Stewarts & Lloyds. Later the company became part of British Steel, until its eventual demise in the late 1990s. A modern industrial complex has now replaced the old works. *(June Connaughton)*

The last pit pony is brought to surface at the Coombs Wood Colliery, 31 May 1952. *(Halesowen Library)*

This very old picture, believed to have been taken on 6 July 1868, is of a meeting of members of the Mine Agents Association of South Staffordshire. It was held at the Blackheath Colliery belonging to Mr W.H. Dawes. *(BCLM)*

The words of William Blake, 'dark satanic mills', spring to mind when considering this portion of Stewarts & Lloyds, seen here in the early 1920s. *(Phyllis Bateman)*

The St John's Ambulance Brigade pictured at the Stewarts & Lloyds Coombs Wood Works, February 1941. The ambulance driver is Baden Rose. *(June Connaughton)*

Much of the output from Stewarts & Lloyds Tube Works was delivered by canal to various parts of the country, and here in the 1970s is the canal boat maintenance area. The boat out of the water on the right is for repair, and the tar heater (with the brick and pipe chimney) can be seen behind boat No. 47. This view looks towards the Coombs Wood tunnel, on the Dudley No. 2 canal. *(Ron Moss)*

The flight of steps leading from Gorsty Hill Road (almost opposite the Old Dun Cow public house), to the private road serving Stewarts & Lloyds Ltd, with the factory in the background, 3 March 1974. *(Halesowen Library)*

In addition to the factory on the BTH site, another to be erected by the Government to manufacture shells for the First World War was the Collins Works in Narrow Lane. At the time of this postcard, perhaps the 1920s, it was almost derelict, but later became Firth Vickers, world-famous manufacturers of stainless steel. It is now demolished and has been replaced by a housing estate. The spare land to the right of the road, yet to receive a surface of tarmac, is now the site of Hurst Green Primary School. *(Ken Rock Collection)*

A group of workers at the Government Cartridge Factory No. 1 (Blackheath), which was later to become BTH Ltd, c. 1920. Back row, left to right: -?-, Lily Neale, Bessie Parkes, -?-, Florrie Limbert, -?-, -?-. Middle row: Mrs Hadley, Mr Ingram, -?-, -?-, -?-. Front row: Mrs Nightingale on the far left is the only name known. *(Ray Parkes)*

A postcard of the BTH works, from the Fairfield Road side, *c.* 1920. *(Ken Rock Collection)*

BTH was acquired by the AEI group of companies and these are the girls who worked in the 'Tag Production' office in 1968–9. Standing. left to right: Betty Parkes, Janet Turner, Jill Rowe, Jane Harris, Susan Bate, Miss Mortimer (forelady), Ann Griffiths, Madge Phillips, Mary Shemwell, Lottie Wilson, Ann Hughes. Kneeling: Ethel Bastable, Maureen Jones, Pat Detheridge, Gladys Trevis. *(Susan Bate)*

Workers of Joseph Wyle & Co., blacksmith, Birmingham Road, early twentieth century. Back row, left to right: -?-, William Bills, Nellie Wyle, David Wyle, Tom Downing. Middle row: Jack Armstrong, Jimmy Hughes, Billy Downing, -?-, Stanley Beese, Frank Parkes, Sam Wyle, Joseph Wyle. Front row: Turk the dog, -?-, Harry Adams, Joe Aldridge, Jimmy Hughes jnr. *(Robert Crumpton)*

Workers at Victoria Engineering Works in Victoria Road pose with a car they are in the process of rebuilding, 1950s. *(Edna Wheeler)*

The workforce at Thomas Gadd, manufacturers of rivets, at their factory in Ross, displaying the tools of their trade. Modern regulations would probably prohibit the two young children from being on the premises, but in the late Victorian/early Edwardian period, when this picture was taken, it was obviously allowed. *(Ann Green)*

Ten employees of Belgrave Engineering, Belgrave Road, who between them had an aggregate of over 300 years' service, qualified for gold watches at a ceremony held in 1982. The Chairman of the Company, C. Henry Pittaway, is seen presenting Mrs Edna Jones with her award. The other recipients were Ivy Skett, Ken Parkes, Jack Tromans, Gertie Wood, Danny Hovells, Cyril Williams, Rhona Dingley, William Davies and Barry Beaman. *(Chris Brettle)*

This lovely picture was taken in the courtyard of the family business of Isaac Williams, who ran a wheelwright and shoeing shop, in Birmingham Road, next to Rose's, the cobbler and shoemaker. Among those pictured are Annie Williams, 'Old Charlie', Joseph Williams and on the left Edgar Baker. *(Vera Basterfield)*

Norman Brettle at work in the 1950s as a carpenter at the building firm of Harper's, who have their headquarters and factory in Beeches Road. *(Amy Bussey)*

Dangerfield and Page, commonly known as the 'Bag Factory' was situated in Belgrave Road, and as the nickname suggests originally made hessian sacks, later on plastic bags. This group of workers, *c.* 1938, includes Mabel Slim, May Robinson, Doris Careless, Kate Woodhouse, Elsie Plant, Mr and Mrs Postones, Sally Jones and Eva White. Mr Postones was a prominent member of the Blackheath Salvation Army. He worked in an outbuilding, where he would wash returning bags to hand over to the girls to re-sew into new sizes, before selling them on to industrial concerns for use as packaging. *(Mary Tromans)*

To celebrate Victory, local firms from Blackheath and Halesowen were invited to put on an exhibition of goods that they had made during the Second World War. This took place at the Borough Hall, Halesowen, in October 1945. Here we see part of the display of electric motors and other materials constructed at the BTH factory. *(Tony Houghton)*

Alan Crompton is hard at work, *c.* 1950, breaking rock in the marl-hole that was situated in Station Road/Oldbury Road, the current site of the Regis Heath Estate. Three men used to work in the quarry obtaining marl to be used in the adjoining brickyard of the Regis Brick Company. The excess split rock was used to build boundary walls and paths in the works perimeter. The bricks produced by Hobbs & Co. were of the highest quality, and were in great demand in the locality and beyond. *(Alan Crompton)*

Ray Jones prepares for work in the marl-hole at Hobbs & Co.'s brickyard. The track used to carry the quarried marl to the surface can be seen clearly. *(Alan Crompton)*

Thomas Gregory, a railway porter who was based at Rowley Regis and Blackheath station in the early 1900s. *(BCLM)*

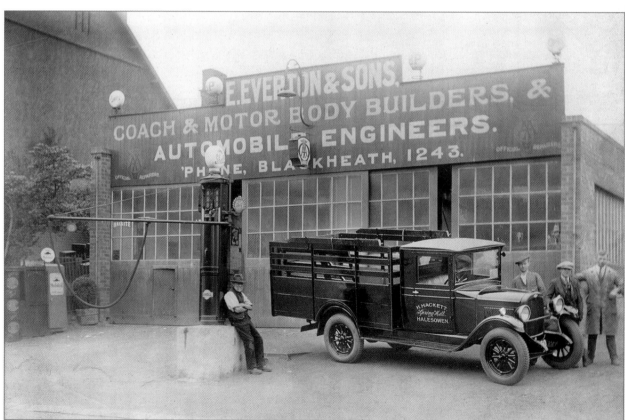

Next to the Conservative Club in Long Lane was Everton's Garage, seen here in about 1940. Here we have Eli Everton on the left and Herbert Everton on the right, with the driver of the lorry and his mate looking on. *(Horace Wilson)*

Mr Harrison (right), the proprietor of Regis
Motors, is seen discussing a deal with Dick Smith
in 1951. *(Lesley Taylor)*

The forecourt and
petrol pumps of Regis
Motors, who
specialised in the sale
of Jowett Javelin cars.
The garage was on
the bridge at the
bottom of Powke
Lane. *(Lesley Taylor)*

A group of workers sneak a few minutes off to pose for a photograph at Pittaway's, 1960s. *(Chris Brettle)*

To the rear of the premises of Marsh & Baxter's butcher shop in High Street were these animal pens and slaughterhouse, seen here in the late 1950s. Access was gained through the entry between two shops, and walls of the pens are still visible in the car park behind today's flower shop. Cliff Sturman and Joseph White are seen tending the animals, which will shortly be on sale as lamb and pork chops! *(John White)*

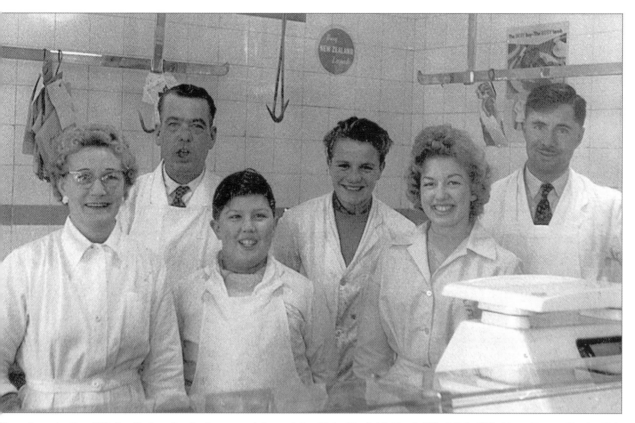

Seen here in the Clift family butcher's shop are, left to right, Elsie Hatfield, Fred Clift, Mick Clift, Tony Brant, Freda Clift and Bob Algar. *(Freda Green)*

Stan White, butcher, is seen in his shop in High Street with Clifford Sturman in the background. The pristine Imperial weights are, of course, one of the sights now unacceptable to the march of progress. *(John White)*

Workers pose outside the shop and factory of Orchard Confectionery in Holly Road in 1927. The premises were demolished, together with the police station which was situated close by, to make way for re-development in the mid-1970s, at one time the ground was scheduled to be used to replace the Victorian premises of Blackheath Infant School, but that scheme was abandoned and currently the area is unused. *(Ann Green)*

The workforce at Orchard Confectionery pose with the firm's delivery van in Holly Road, sometime between 1925 and 1930. *(Ann Green)*

Several generations of young ladies learned first aid and nursing skills from their involvement in the local St. John's Ambulance cadets unit; here they are being taught infant welfare skills, *c.* 1960. Amy Brettle, at the extreme right of the picture, dedicated her life to this, and several other charitable institutions, including the Soldiers, Sailors and Air Force Association, and was a prominent member of High Street Methodist Church and a number of local choral societies. *(County Express)*

A scene from the 1960 Works Gala, held on the BTH sports field, showing parents and children lining up for a ride on the miniature railway. The old cottages in Yates Lane are visible in the background. *(Charles Morgan)*

The Hill & Cakemore Infant Welfare Clinic held annual garden parties on the recreation ground belonging to BTH Ltd in Cakemore Road. The mothers and babies, together with the welfare workers assembled at their meeting place (the schoolroom of the Congregational church in Green Lane) and made their way to the sports ground through the local streets. Here the decorated prams are seen leading the procession, with the car of the Medical Officer, on the way to the celebration, Thursday 5 June 1930. *(Margaret Andersson)*

Mothers and children from the Hill & Cakemore Infant Welfare group, during baby week 1930. They are at the Kings Theatre (Long Lane) where they have been invited for a free film show on Wednesday 4 June, at 2pm, by kind permission of the proprietor, T. Cooper. The films which they were shown included *Drifting, Motherhood, Giro the Germ,* and *The Work of the Welfare Centre.* 'Topical News' and a talkie were shown afterwards. *(Margaret Andersson)*

On Friday 6 June 1930 a party of thirty-five mothers and children, together with the infant welfare nurses, visited the Midland Counties Dairies, Birmingham, for a demonstration of the latest techniques of milk production. They are seen in the picture above about to board the coach outside their headquarters in Green Lane, and in the picture below posing in the Corporation Street depot. They were given lectures about milk collection from farms near the city, processing details and the four brands of milk produced. Afterwards the mothers were entertained to a feast of ice-cream and the babies sampled the highest grade milk, while the nurses were escorted around the laboratories. *(Margaret Andersson)*

Bethesda Sports, a football team formed from Hackett Street Sunday School scholars, who had their headquarters at the church. They played in the Cradley Heath and Oldbury Leagues. Back row, left to right: Jack Taylor (mascot), Ernie Perry, Ted Baker, Harry Moseley, Job Taylor, Len Hadley, Albert Poole, Denis Sidaway (Hon. Sec.). Front row: A. Taylor, Stan Priest, Arthur Faulkner (Captain), Reggie Watton, Albert Harvey. *(Eric Parkes)*

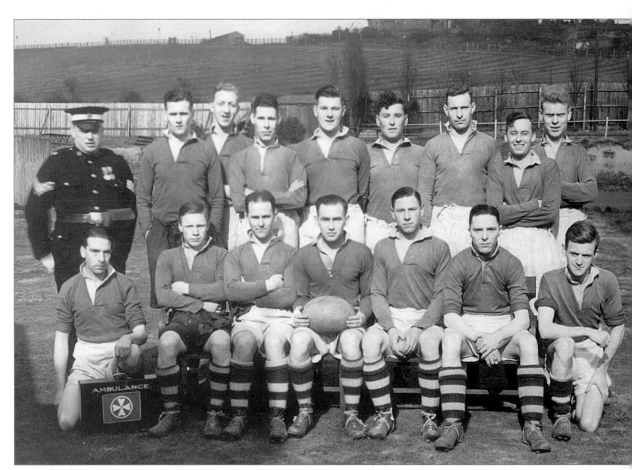

Stewarts & Lloyds Rugby Team on their playing field at the bottom of Gorsty Hill, mid-1930s. The ploughed fields in the background indicate the lack of industrial development which today covers the area. Bert Townsend, a keen sportsman, is second from left on the back row. He worked for S&L at Coombs Wood, moving to their Birmingham office before eventually transferring to the Glasgow branch on his marriage in 1948. *(Elsie Scarrott)*

The waste ground known to generations as 'The Quack' was 'all things to all men' at different times and seasons. The water-filled marl-hole was a popular fishing ground, and an early version of Moto-cross took place with bikes on the tracks around the perimeter. In winter it was a (rough) football pitch, and in summer even Lords could not compare with the cricketing activities. Here we see a serious game taking place in 1950, with, left to right, Jim 'Spud' Taylor, Ray White, Brian Hall and Keith Plunkett. *(Graham Beasley)*

Another, but quite different event, on the same playing field was a cricket tournament, held between the factories of BTH Ltd at Blackheath and Newcastle. Here we see the two competing teams who played in the 1952 match. *(Tony Houghton)*

The men who made up the Blackheath Harriers, in 1913–14. *(Black Country Bugle)*

Mrs Mary Hollies is seen distributing medals and prizes to children who had taken part in the Coronation celebrations in Garland Crescent and Summerfields Avenue, 1953. Here it is the turn of Janet Mole to receive hers, watched over by other residents of the street. *(Charles Male)*

Taking the epic flights of Amy Johnson as their example, members of the Hobbs family and friends are seen doing their part in the fundraising activities for the Blackheath Carnival in the 1930s. Madge Bussey is in cockpit of the plane, with her husband Bill at the front right. Ben Hobbs, Duncan Gadd and Enoch Hobbs are standing at the left. (*Maisie Hayman*)

A couple of generations later the carnival is now called the Blackheath Gala, and local children, encouraged by parents, are taking place in a race held at Britannia Park on 21 September 1963. (*County Express*)

The Blackheath Town Band with their instruments outside High Street Methodist Church, mid-1920s. The gentleman out of uniform in the centre is the well-known local figure Ben Hobbs. *(Margaret Patrick)*

For a comparatively small place Blackheath had a wide range of musical associations. This is a production of an operetta at Birmingham Road Methodist Church between 1920 and 1930. *(Lily Knowles)*

Blackheath Operatic Society gave their public performances at The Kings Theatre, and this group shows some of the cast of *The Country Girl*, which was staged at some point between 1930 and 1933. *(Edna Wheeler)*

A scene from the Blackheath Operatic Society performance of *The Desert Song*, which was given at The Kings Theatre during the early 1930s. The locals flocked to see the lavish productions. Some of those on stage are Frank Webster (in uniform on the left), Nora Bennett, Edgar Bloomer and Bob Wheeler. *(Edna Wheeler)*

A meeting of the National British Women's Total Abstinence Union (which was commonly called the British Women's Temperance League) at the house in Ross owned by the old lady at the extreme right of the second row down, *c.* 1910. It is believed that many of these ladies had a connection with High Street Methodist Church. Several members of the Hobbs family are in the picture, including Gladys (kneeling at the left of the front row), Edith, Laura and Lily (top row, third, fourth and fifth from left). Also included are Annie Green, Rene Smith, Ivy and Winnie Evans). *(Maisie Hayman)*

Being almost as far from the sea as is possible, parties of Blackheath residents took every opportunity to take holidays or day trips. Here we see a group taking the air in an open top charabanc on a trip to Weston-Super-Mare in 1927. Among the passengers are John Parkes (standing) and Lily Parkes, with Geoff Parkes and Mrs Neale. *(Ray Parkes)*

For many years the Adelphi Dance Studio, on the corner of Masters Lane, was the place for young people (and those not so young) to learn the latest rhythms. In May 1957 a group is assembled to celebrate the birthday of one of the instructors, Frank, who is seated on the floor in the centre of the picture. The other teacher was Dorothy Hipkiss at the left of the photograph. Others include Jimmy Taylor, Johnny Howard, Jennifer Cox, Jane Lawley, Rita Russon, Margaret Hodges, Gordon Bennett, Gillian Partridge and Reg Cullwick. *(Gill Rawle)*

A group of ladies meeting at Tiffany's Night Club, formerly the Odeon Cinema, Long Lane, for their keep fit club, 1970s. Among those pictured are Mabel Smith, Doreen Fellows, Rita Butroid, Margaret Cohen. *(Mabel Smith)*

Members of the Hill & Cakemore Welfare Section of Civil Defence are seen on a training exercise on 5 October 1957, learning how to make a bread oven. This picture is printed with acknowledgement to the Ministry of Agriculture, Fisheries and Food. *(Halesowen Library)*

A rare picture taken inside the Pavilion Cinema in High Street when it was being used as a dance hall in the 1960s. The people shown, including Prudence Batson on the front row, acted as the organising committee for a variety of events which were held there. *(Alan Crompton)*

4

Shops, Pubs & Clubs

A fine display of china and silverware can be seen in the window of this shop at 108 High Street, *c.* 1924. Ellen Hobbs is on the right and her daughter-in-law Doris (who was the wife of William E. Hobbs) on the left. Will later took over the running of the shop, and also had a delivery round in the surrounding area. *(Maisie Hayman)*

Mrs Southall on the doorstep of the family hardware and locksmith business in High Street, 1920s. The wide range of items available for sale indicates the developing importance of the town, not only to local people, but also to those further afield. The business eventually passed into the hands of Ashfield's, who have maintained the premises, and skills, in the provision of security services and hardware to the present day. *(Jill Bromley)*

Below: Early in the twentieth century the original George and Dragon public house in High Street was this building, much smaller than today's establishment of the same name, seen here in winter-time. The landlord, 'Sergeant' Salt, is pictured in front of the main entrance with the drinking trough in the foreground, to which patrons would tie their horses while partaking of refreshments. On the left of the picture is the fish and chip shop belonging to another well-known character, 'Tally-Ho', who also sold vegetables and herbs around the town from a large wickerwork basket. One of the older parts of town, recalling more rural days, is Shepherd's Fold, which lies to the left of these buildings. *(Author's Collection)*

In keeping with the Art-Nouveau style of the time, the haberdashery store of Jane Eley underwent a facelift in the 1930s, and remained like this until the late 1990s. *(Ros Hill)*

The wool shop in Halesowen Street, first established in 1920, was run until closure (because of the redevelopment scheme) by Alice Downing. *(Robert Downing)*

Mrs Maria Willetts, wife of the founder, is seen here outside the sweet shop at 59 High Street, early 1930s. Mr Willetts was a master sugar boiler, and conducted a wholesale and retail business, with the factory situated in the yard up the entry. As can be seen from the sign the company was established in 1870, and delighted many generations of children with the variety of goods produced. Visible in the window is one of the specialities, a large stick of rock: especially popular at Christmas were those shaped like walking sticks. Also produced were confections made in the shape of floral baskets, and other designs. In this picture the shop is decorated to support the Blackheath Carnival, as can be seen from the poster of the left, inviting patrons to guess the weight of goods at 2d a go. Although presently trading as a convenience store, the premises remain much the same today. (Dorothy Parkes)

T.P. Moyle & Co. was a chain of grocery shops, with many branches in the Black Country. This is the store on the corner of High Street and Heath Street in the mid-1950s. The staff here are, left to right, Mr R. Field, Mrs A. Parkes, Mrs Arthur, Mr Haden (manager), Mr J. Horton and Mr G. Willetts. It was a time for great patriotism, as can be seen from the posters urging customers to 'Think of England and Yourself First', 'All goods in this window are produced by British labour', and a display of Moyle's English Cheddar cheese. *(Margaret Harris)*

Customers look through the window at the stock in the showroom of John T. Harris, in Birmingham Road, late 1960s. The bookmaking premises of Reg Clee and Fred Darby's grocery shop can be seen on the opposite side of the road. *(Paul Harris)*

ituated in Nimmings Road, close to the Shell Corner island was Jack's Bazaar, pictured in about 1960, proudly isplaying the range of goods available. It is now a carpet warehouse. *(Bill Sampson)*

he Acorn public
ouse, in Cocksheds
ane at the junction
vith Malt Mill Lane,
on 14 July 1974.
'or several years it
as stood as an
mpty shell.
Halesowen Library)

The Anchor Inn, Coombs Road,
3 March 1974. In recent years it has
been re-named The Lighthouse, and
is well known for the mural that
decorates the exterior.
(*Halesowen Library*)

Mr Parkes and his family on the steps of
their shop at 19 High Street, *c.* 1850.
As can be seen from the shopfront he was
a general dealer, yet the window is
displaying violins and banjos among
other items, indicating that he must have
had a special interest in musical
instruments. (*BCLM*)

The billboard indicates the site in Halesowen Street that Mitchells & Butlers were about to use for re-building the Britannia Inn, late 1920s. The old houses in Hackett Street (Heath Street) and the Methodist chapel can be seen in the background. *(CHAS)*

With construction completed, the new Britannia Inn is pictured at its opening on 8 December 1930. Apart from a few face-lifts over the years the structure is virtually identical in this century, now trading as part of the J.D. Wetherspoon chain. *(CHAS)*

Although the picture on the previous page indicates only minor external changes, the lounge bar of the newly opened Britannia public house in Halesowen Street was quite different from its successor. *(CHAS)*

The outdoor off-licence at 73 Birmingham Road, 28 June 1960. The building to the left was at the time the gas showroom, later to become the shop and studio of Charles Male (photographer), with the long-established family butcher's firm of Levett's next door to the right. *(Author's Collection)*

The buildings named Hathaway House, built in 1905, which stand at the junction of Long Lane with Green Lane, June 1974. On the corner is the greengrocer's business of Walter Hingley. To the right is the forecourt of the Esso garage, the Blackheath branch of the locally famous Bells Motors, with headquarters at the top of Mucklow Hill, and next door is the entrance to the Midland Counties milk depot. *(Halesowen Library)*

The draper and hosier shop operated by the Whitehouse family, in Halesowen Street. *(Frances Dolphin)*

Members of the Hill & Cakemore Conservative Club, Long Lane, are seen celebrating their annual dinner at The King's Highway Hotel, 1950s. Among those present are Cis and Harold Partridge, and Ron and Nellie Harris. *(Yvonne Grant)*

The award-winning snooker and billiards team from the Blackheath Liberal Club poses outside the club in John Street, 29 April 1928. *(June Connaughton)*

The Bell Inn, Gorsty Hill, with Samuel Lowe, and dog, 1920s. *(Elsie Scarrott)*

Ansells have taken over from Mitchells and Butlers at The Bell Inn in this photograph taken on 3 March 1974. In recent years the name has been changed to The Bell and Bear, and it is a popular place. *(Halesowen Library)*

Nos 299–302 Long Lane, right on the island at the Shell Corner, 28 April 1974. The long-established Riley's Drug Stores takes centre position. *(Halesowen Library)*

Before opening their shop opposite The George and Dragon (*see* pp. 76–7), the Willetts family ran a confectionery business at the bottom of the High Street, roughly where the Midland Bank is now situated. Originally a cycle dealer's (old fading advertisements are visible on the wall above the name sign), it was decided that there was more future in sweet making. One of the large walking stick rocks can be seen at the left of the window display. The girl is Mercy Willetts, and she is with her mother, Maria. *(Dorothy Parkes)*

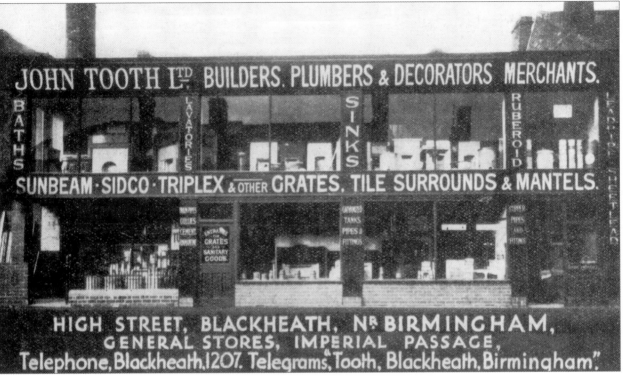

An old advertisment from the 1920s for John Tooth Ltd, High Street, the long-established builders' merchants. *(Author's Collection)*

Jim Bolton is seen outside his painting and decorating shop on the left-hand side of Long Lane (when going towards the Stag) at the Shell Corner. *(David Hassall)*

Kath Williams outside Parkes's wallpaper shop, which faced the traffic island in central Blackheath. Kath was about nineteen or twenty at the time of the picture, dated about 1939 or 1940, and she died aged seventy-eight in July 1999. Mr Parkes snr had two sons in the business, with shops at Brierley Hill and Cradley Heath. The latter was run by his son Cyril, who retired to live at Clent Hall. *(William Blunt)*

Represented by a store in the High Street was the grocery chain belonging to Maypole Dairy Company Limited, who, long before the advent of the modern supermarket chains, retailed many of their own branded products. Advertised here in 1926 are Maypole tea, Maypole butter and Maypole margarine. The grocer on the left is Jim Bubb. *(Geoffrey Bubb)*

Almost opposite the
shop of Mr Bolton
(*see* p. 87), was the
shop of James Hobbs,
renowned, as the sign
says, for selling
almost anything.
Ruby Compton, the
daughter of James,
is seen arranging
some of the stock.
(Maisie Hayman)

Standing in isolation after the adjacent
properties have been demolished, the
Mother & Baby shop in Birmingham Road
is holding its closing down sale, *c.* 1972.
To the right of the picture are the backs of
the remaining properties in Oldbury Road.
(Author)

The Blackheath Liberal Club boasted not only sporting teams (*see* p. 84), but also had a concert party, who are pictured here in John Street in the mid-1920s. Baden Rose is second from the left. (*June Connaughton*)

The Pavilion Cinema and dance hall was turned into Pearks Supermarket, the first self-service grocery store on the High Street in the early 1960s. The local offices of the *Birmingham Post and Mail* are visible at the right edge of the picture. After several years trading under various companies the premises fell into disuse. The interior was eventually completely altered in the mid-1990s, and turned into the local neighbourhood office for Sandwell Social Services Department. (*Alan Crompton*)

5

Churches & Chapels

Birmingham Road Methodist Church and schoolroom from Causeway, shortly after the Sunday
School had been completed in 1932. At this time there was nothing standing on the opposite
corner behind the fence, where eventually a block of offices was constructed for
Leonard Smith & Co., chemical manufacturers. *(Ken Rock Collection)*

Recently demolished, the Mission Church of St Ambrose, daughter church of St Paul's, stood just off Gorsty Hill on land adjacent to the Stewarts & Lloyds factory. This group photograph shows the clergy, organist and choir in the early 1930s. *(Elsie Scarrott)*

Mrs Ivy Hall, one of the Sunday School teachers at Heath Street Methodist Church, arranges a floral display on the altar following the opening of the new church in September 1976. Among those in the picture are Eric Parkes, Arthur Hall and Clive Temple. *(Ivy Hall)*

or many years High Street Methodist Church ran a flourishing Boys Brigade Company; in 1932 when this picture was taken they were designated the 1st South Staffs Company. One of the highlights of the year was, and still is, the annual Camp, and the boys, together with officers and helpers are seen at Ludlow, with the smartly erected tents in the background. The Captain was John Siviter, seen in the flat hat towards the left, standing next to his wife Annie-Maria. *(Clarence Siviter)*

A new Methodist church was opened in Birchfield Lane, at Whiteheath, on 30 June 1956, and here the former minister, the Revd John T. Gray (under whose leadership the plans had been realised), receives the keys from the architect, Stanley Griffiths, in the presence of the mayor and mayoress of Oldbury. Among the others present are the Revd W.W. Ion (the current minister), Fred Evans, George Round and Tom Willetts. *(County Express)*

Birmingham Road Methodist Church frequently held garden parties to provide a social function and to raise money for church funds. This particular occasion was in 1968, in the grounds of Olive House, Halesowen Street, the home of Fred and Emily Ingram. The young couple with the pram are the Revd John and Mrs Jean Hope, who were part of the ministerial team at the time. Also visible are Fred Honeysett, Jim Parry and Don Payne. *(Author)*

Three couples, Joseph and Frances Poole, Fred and Edith Adams and Walter and Olive Wootton were all married by the Revd George Frogatt at Birmingham Road Methodist Church during April 1928, and they celebrated their Golden Weddings by inviting more than 200 people to a celebration at the church. They had all retained their connection with the church in a variety of ways. Back row, left to right: the Revd George Price, Mr Wootton, Mr Adams, Mr Poole, the Revd Wilfred Burton, the Revd Reginald Parsons, Mrs Burton. Front row: Mrs Price, Mrs Wootton, Mrs Adams, Mrs Poole, Mrs Parsons. *(Author)*

At the same garden party as on the previous page, pictured outside the greenhouse are John and Kathleen Johnson. John worked at Birmetals in Woodgate, was an accomplished cricketer, and held many offices in the life of the Methodist Church. A noted local preacher, he was for many years an active member of the Methodist Local Preacher's Mutual Aid Association, and went on to become its national president. *(Author)*

One of the two Methodist churches situated in Malt Mill Lane, this is the interior of the Cocksheds Church, just before it closed on 8 October 1995 to join with others to form the new Central Methodist Church. *(Author)*

The Methodist church in Beeches Road (now used as headquarters for the Loyal Order of Moose) had a youth club and members Fred Archer, George Bennett, Ernie Parkes, Walter Tom, Billy Taylor, George Webster, Evelyn Archer, Eileen Pratt, Iris Lowe, Madge Shaw and Lilian ? are seen with their Minister, the Revd George Yates. *(Madge Lyman)*

Hurst Green Methodist Church was founded in 1890 and originally met in this building, which was in Hurst Green Road. The congregation moved to Narrow Lane when the church was built in 1900, later constructing the new building in 1936. Currently there is a plan to extend the church to meet the needs of the present generation. *(Rita Shaw)*

Above: The Blackheath Salvation Army Band (commonly known as 'Eli's Band') outside the Citadel in Park Street, early 1920s. Back row, left to right: H. Bateman, W. Stevenson, B. Stevenson, Mr Carr, Mr Coley, B. Knott, F. Patrick, A. Bagnall, J. Tromans. Middle row: A. Bagnall snr, J. Meredith, B. Lowe, W. Patrick, R. Meredith, Mr Siviter. Front row: J. Parkes, G. Hill, R. Hill, J. Robinson, D. Smith, Eli Siviter, B. Meredith, R. Plant, H. Robinson, J. Rock. Seated on the pavement: J. Bagnall (left) and G. Skett. *(Margaret Patrick)*

On 3 March 1975 a service was held at the Malt Mill Lane Methodist Church to celebrate the work of four Sunday School workers who between them had clocked up 159 years of dedicated service. Here we see Albert Tyldesley admiring his Long Service Certificate presented by the National Christian Education Council for fifty-three years work, much of it as Superintendent. Others to receive awards were Lucy Edwards for forty years, Nellie Edwards (forty years) and Reg Harris (twenty-six years). *(Joyce Bennett)*

An outing of families from the Elim Church, Cardale Street, to Trentham Gardens, Staffordshire, early 1960s. Among the adults identified are Patrick Mohan, Violet Handley, Phoebe Handley, Rebecca Spittle, Freda Millwood and Mrs Cowdrey (wife of the the Minister). The children include Graham and Keith Handley. *(Donald Handley)*

Mr Charles Gostelow presents a Bible to Mrs Winifred Knott (right), at a service held at Hurst Green Methodist Churc on 5 February 1955 to welcome her as local President of the Local Preachers' Mutual Aid Association. Ernest Wyl local preachers' secretary, is in the centre. *(County Express)*

Outside the Congregational Church and Sunday School, showing the Long Lane/Green Lane junction, and Colliers Row of cottages in the background, *c.* 1920. Left to right: Mary Walker (Davis), Edith Walker, Evelyn Harries, Gladys Harries, Mary Hall (later Kite), Florence Crump, Rose Moore, Joseph Adams (choirmaster), the Revd W.J. Harries, Tom Kite, Harry Ashfield, Joe Moore, Cliff Kite, George Bishop, Sam Westwood, George Gregory. *(Ray Parkes)*

To commemorate those who had been associated with Malt Mill Lane Methodist Church and had been killed in the First World War, this memorial plaque was dedicated in 1921. Those remembered were Leonard Bastable, Thomas Bowater, Joseph Tibbetts, Walter Brookes, Bertie Cox and Ernest Tildesley. *(Ken Rock Collection)*

The young people's class at Beeches Road Methodist Church, some time between 1925 and 1930. *(Margaret Fereday)*

Philip Bromley and Sam Parkes with the banner from Waterfall Lane Mission Hall, which was actually situated in Tory Street (later to be renamed Grange Road). Dated about 1930, this picture was taken on ground off Waterfall Lane, now the site of the large Higgs Field Estate, at one of the annual treats. *(Geoffrey Bubb)*

The 2nd Blackheath Company of the Girls Life Brigade pictured outside High Street Methodist Church, 1947.
(Nellie Holloway)

Scouts and Guides from the region meet at
St Paul's Church for a Thanksgiving Day Service,
23 February 1963. Among those troops
represented are 1st Rowley, 1st Hill & Cakemore,
and 1st Lapal. *(CHAS)*

Whiteheath Methodist Church held a fund-raising bazaar in 1955, and the minister of the day, the Revd William W. Ion, is seen next to his wife, along with members of the church and Sunday School. *(CHAS)*

Samuel Parkes, who died on 16 February 1915 at the age of seventy-eight, a life-long member of Birmingham Road Methodist Church. His memorial inside the church states that 'He was devoted to this church and its institutions. He was a Trustee, Leader, Sunday School Superintendent and Choirmaster (a position he held for 58 years)'. *(Author's Collection)*

6

People & Events

Ben Adams (nicknamed 'Benny Wacker') was a second-hand dealer, with shop premises next to Blackheath Market and storage sheds in Ashley Street. He was a stalwart of High Street Methodist Church for many years. *(Charles Male)*

The wedding of Bill Bussey and Emily Hobbs, which had taken place at High Street Methodist Church, 25 September 1921. Back row, left to right: John Parkes, Mr and Mrs Hackett, Enoch Hobbs, Mr Morgan, the Revd Robert Curzon, -?-. Middle row: Mr and Mrs. Bussey, Ivan Weston, Billy Bussey, Emily Bussey, Elizabeth Hobbs, Jane Parkes, Benjamin Hobbs. Front row: Eleanor Hobbs, Mrs Belcher (or Dingley), Mary Hobbs, Dorothy Hobbs, Ellen Hobbs, Victor Hobbs, Cyril Bussey(?) (Maisie Hayman)

Julia Whitehouse is seen here with the firm's horse-drawn dray, delivering milk to the Blackheath area in the 1930s. She is outside the premises of Miss Gladys Robson, the well-known lady photographer, in High Street (almost opposite The George & Dragon). The Whitehouse family had a dairy farm and milk business which was based in Causeway Green. (George Whitehouse)

Above: Ernest Henry Careless in front of his cottage in Oldbury Road, where he had lived since about 1920. Mr Careless worked as a tube fittings screwer for fifty-six years, and together with his two sons looked after the gardens and later ran a garden centre. The cypress trees form a particular feature, and at one time they were particularly proud of a strain of pea which grew to a height of over 8 feet, the seeds for which are now unobtainable in this country. *(Dennis Careless)*

The Willetts family owned a sweet shop, situated on the corner of Avenue Road and Long Lane, and three young men about town are pictured in the yard behind the shop, *c.* 1930. On the left is Samuel Willetts and on the right is Edgar Bloomer, but the identity of the young man in the centre is not known. *(Chris Willetts)*

Mr and Mrs Smith, parents of Jack (*see* p. 111) are seen outside the family home at the corner of Birmingham Road and Mackmillan Road, together with Dorothy and Dulcie, 1940s. In the background the old cottages, now replaced with elderly persons dwellings, and the thriving shop, still standing, are visible. *(Freda Smith)*

William Mason (centre, back row) was a Trustee and Superintendent of Hackett Street Methodist Church in the early 1900s. His daughter Alice, front row, was a Sunday School teacher, and Joseph Law (front) was a teacher, a fine local preacher, who emigrated to America in about 1912. *(Eric Parkes)*

John Dallow, JP, CC (Staffs) was born on 17 June 1851 and died on 12 October 1923. For over fifty years was closely associated to the Birmingham Road Methodist Church and Sunday School. He attended as a scholar in the school, became a teacher and afterwards secretary. He was a keen church member, trustee, leader and was always keenly interested in its welfare and progress. In working life he was a master builder, and had his own construction company in the town. *(Author's Collection)*

To mark the Coronation of HM Queen Elizabeth II, the children of Hurst Green held a celebration party, and are pictured here in fancy dress outside Wright's dairy in Fairfield Road. The adults at the rear are Mr Brookes, -?-, Mrs Wright and Mrs Dutton. The boy with bicycle on the left is Graham Brookes, and some of the others identified are as follows: Back row: Michael Lee, Pauline Farmer, Pat Hovells, Tony Hutchinson. Third row: Peter Tibbetts, Christopher Mole, Pat Willetts, Mabel Fox. Second row: Elizabeth Wakefield, Christine Hovells Suzanne Dutton, Roger Hingley, Shan Lappage, Judy Lappage. Front row: Roger Wakefield, Mary Farmer, Carol Jennings, Victoria Dutton, Joyce Taylor. *(Mary Hollis)*

In April 1950 members of the Blackheath Orchestral Society held a party in the schoolroom of High Street Methodis
Church, to celebrate their twenty-first birthday. The Society had been started in 1929 by Alfred E. Adams and seven o
his friends, their first rehearsal being on 10 May of that year. As well as providing accompaniment for the High Stree
Choral Society, they performed many concerts for charity. Mr Adams is seated on the front row, with his wife and the
minister of the time, the Revd Percy Myers. *(Dorothy Phillips)*

The road is closed, a make-shift bonfire has been constructed and bunting decorates the houses in Habberley Road. Local residents celebrate the end of the Second World War on VE Day. *(Irene Pritchard)*

Crowds gathered in Halesowen Street to mark the opening of new branch of Carter's Electronic, when Peter Adamson (famous as Len Fairclough of *Coronation Street*) performed the ceremony. He is seen here shaking hands with Councillor Evelyn Matthews, and brothers Gordon and Reg Carter are on the right-hand side. *(Gordon Carter)*

ck Smith, who was the Mayor of Sandwell in 1984–5.
e lived most of his life in Birmingham Road, and was
ctively involved in the Trade Union movement before
eing elected to Warley and subsequently Sandwell
ouncils. During his period as mayor the Borough of
andwell was twinned with the town of Le Blanc Mesnil,
n the outskirts of Paris. *(Freda Smith)*

lifford Harris on the piano accompanies Joseph Southall on the violin as they rehearse in High Street Methodist
choolroom, early 1920s. *(Jill Bromley)*

A few years after the picture on p. 110 the bunting is once more in evidence in Habberley Road. This time it is 195
and the occasion is the Coronation of the Queen. *(Gwen Davies)*

Nellie Payne, Annie Payne and Mary Payne outside the family draper's shop in Halesowen Street, 1947. *(Nellie Holloway*

group of children who
belonged to the Saturday
morning picture clubs, meeting
at both the Rex and King's
cinemas, were lucky enough to
travel to the Birmingham
Hippodrome to meet one of their
all-time favourite screen western
performers, Roy Rogers. Roy,
with his wife Dale Evans, is seen
here with a group including
Keith Davies (extreme right).
The event took place in the
mid-1950s. *(Keith Davies)*

Decimus Gaunt can truly be described as one of the characters of old Blackheath. He was publican of The Old Bush Revived in Powke Lane, and his hostelry was one of the favourites of the many miners, chain and nail makers and factory hands from the town. Married twice, he had thirteen children, the eldest son being Percival, the founder of the famous undertaking business. This picture is of the wedding of Dora, one of his daughters, and Decimus can be seen standing in the centre, next to the bridegroom. *(Peter Gaunt)*

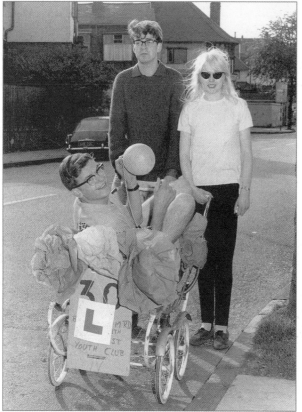

Above: Mrs Rose with her friend Millie Guest on the Causeway in the early 1920s. The building behind them, reaching the pavement, was the original Ebenezer Chapel of Birmingham Road Methodist Church, taken down to make way for the schoolroom in 1923. The neighbourhood was served by the busy family shop opposite the chapel. *(June Connaughton)*

On 9 September 1967 the Birmingham Association of Methodist Youth Clubs organised a sponsored pram push around the 26 miles of the Birmingham Outer Circle bus route to raise funds for missionary work. Birmingham Road Youth Club were represented by Robert Smith (in the pram) with his brother Martin and Gillian Bryant, later to become Mrs Martin Smith. *(Author)*

lderman Ben Hobbs, the first charter mayor of Rowley Regis, and his mayoress Mrs Elizabeth Hobbs, pictured in the
eremonial robes in September 1933. Mr Hobbs was a well-known industrialist and employer in the town, and one of his
rm's showrooms, at the top of Causeway and High Street, remained a landmark until quite recently. *(Maisie Hayman)*

he charter that granted Rowley Regis its status as a borough council, was presented at a ceremony in Old Hill by
George Lansbury MP (then the leader of the Labour Party). This was followed by a procession, led by the Mace Bearer,
round the perimeter of the new Borough, and is seen here as it makes its way along Birmingham Road, going
wards Rowley Church. *(CHAS)*

Marion Woolvin outside the family sweet shop at the top end of High Street, 1930s. *(Maisie Hayman)*

Four generations of James Adams pictured in the garden at the home of Mr Adams snr in Beeches Road, *c.* 1930. *(James Adams)*

o mark the eightieth birthday f Mr Alfred Adams a family arty was organised at Perry ark Road. This photograph ncludes members of the xtended family. Back row, left right: Charles, Alfred, Clara, larence, Geoff, Horace (with 1anty). Middle row: Margaret, onnie, Eric, Edith, Peggy, orothy. Front row: Philip, 1argaret, Ruth, Alfred dams, Derek, Cynthia. Dorothy Phillips)

The children from Causeway, Regis Road and the locality pose in the grounds of The George and Dragon at their party o celebrate the Coronation, 1953. *(Keith Davies)*

Although apparently kitted out in military uniform, these men are members of the Stewarts and Lloyds St John Ambulance Brigade, while on camp in Yarmouth, 1912. *(Elsie Scarrott)*

Blackheath Branch Library in Carnegie Road was re-opened after alterations and redecorations in July 1968. Left to right: Miss A.M. Price (Borough Librarian), Mrs S.V. Ostler and Miss G. Hemmings (Library Assistants), Mrs V.W. Wakeman (Mayoress), Councillor J.P. Padden (Vice-Chairman, Libraries Committee), Councillor V.W. Wakeman (Mayor), Councillor D. Underhill, Mr J. Hickman (Maintenance Section). *(County Express)*

our generations of the sweet-making Willetts family – Ruth Harris (daughter), Martha Willetts, Neil (great randson), Kathleen (grand-daughter). *(Dorothy Parkes)*

. Payne (looking rather dour with his trumpet, seated in the centre of the picture), with four other musicians at live Hill Farm, Hill & Cakemore, *c.* 1920. *(Ken Rock Collection)*

Annie Payne in her draper's shop at 135 Halesowen Street, which opened in the early 1930s. She was noted f
selling many of her goods on credit, as money was rather tight. *(Nellie Holloway)*

A fine selection of paper hats is evident as the children of Hackett Street (Heath Street) occupy the trestle tables erected to mark VE Day. The four lads facing the camera are, left to right: Geoff Bubb, Brian Aldridge, Brian Bubb, and Albert Townsend. *(Geoffrey Bubb)*

he firm of T.W. Lench marked the end of the First World War
y holding a celebration and remembrance party for the men
f Blackheath who had been on active duty. Among those
resent were members of the Hobbs family, who are seated on
e fourth table from the front Third, fourth and fifth from the
ft are William Hobbs and his nephews Ernie (Royal Navy)
nd Enoch (Royal Flying Corps). *(Maisie Hayman)*

ressed here in a distinctive astrakhan jacket, Charles Parrish
as the organist at High Street Methodist Church for several
ears. He was a noted musician who tragically died in 1921
a motorcycle accident in Mucklow Hill. *(Author's Collection)*

John T. Harris is seen with his furniture van, mid-1960s. He had a retail outlet in Birmingham Road, and also ran h own upholstery business in Station Road Old Hill. In due course the business relocated to its present place, the form schoolroom of Birmingham Road Church, where it is now run by his sons, Stephen and Paul. *(Paul Harris)*

Ben Adams is seen with members of his family at the rear of his second-hand shop in the Market Place Blackheath c. 1923. The group consists of Ben, wife Eliza, daughter Ivy, and grandchildren Harry, Daphne, Robert, Ben, Ivy ar Charles. *(Sheila Brookes)*

group of local workmen pose on the steps of the
uilding situated at the corner of Masters Lane and
olt Road, 1905. The two men identified on the right
f the front row are both named Ike Tromans (father
nd son). The premises are currently occupied by
on's Café. *(Ray Parkes)*

he Girls Brigade at High Street Methodist Church form a guard of honour at the wedding of their captain, Una
Villetts, who married Edward McGreal on 20 June 1965. The Minister in the background is the Revd Harold Cope,
ho conducted the service, and among the girls are Chris Willetts and Lorraine Eley. *(Chris Chambers)*

The Oldbury firm of Chance Brothers Ltd had a convalescent home for the employees at their chemical works. Th
was at the top of Narrow Lane. Although only a few miles from the works, the clear fresh air of what is now Hur
Green was a contrast to the polluted air of Oldbury. The rear of the large house looked out on to ground which is no
used as a cemetery by the City of Birmingham. This postcard shows two of the matrons, along with canine friend, i
about 1908. *(Ken Rock Collection)*

Pictured in Marlow Street in 1955, in front of the delivery van of Horace Hopewell, the renowned Blackheath baker, is Eric Parkes, aged fourteen. It is a reminder that boys often helped out with a variety of local firms in order to earn a few pennies as pocket money. *(Eric Parkes)*

Younger members of High Street Methodist Church, thought to be members of the Band of Hope, in fancy dress at a function in the early part of the twentieth century. John Siviter (extreme right) is the only one identified, but the elaborate dress indicates a considerable amount of preparation by parents. There is a distinct patriotic theme, with Britannia taking pride of place and Scots and Welsh ladies in attendance, while many of the boys have opted for military uniforms. *(Clarence Siviter)*

Members of Heath Street Chapel on an outing, 1920s. Left to right: Ivy Yates, Freda Simmons, Lois Parkes, Joe Whorton, Hilda Harper, Phyllis Basterfield, Dolly Mucklow, -?-, -?-, John Brown. *(Eric Parkes)*

With the tea urn to the fore, the tables are ready for action as residents of Terrace Street celebrate VE Day in 1945. *(Margaret Guest)*

A young Keith Davies with his parents Bill and Hilda in the back garden of 32 Causeway with the spire of the church in the background, 1954. Mr Davies was a noted horticulturist in his spare time from working in the Fire Service, and Mrs Davies was for many years an usherette in the local cinemas. *(Keith Davies)*

A group of Blackheath mothers and toddlers, plus a few grandmothers, who went on a trip to Lilleshall Hall in 1949. Back row, left to right : Alice Willetts, May ?, Ivy Windsor, Mrs. Downing, -?-, -?-, Bertha Rose, Mrs Payne, Mrs Smith, Mrs Jones, Enid George, -?-, -?-. Middle row: Mrs Kathleen Johnson, Hilda Hopkins, -?-, -?-, Cath Wright, Kath Mole, Lily Smith, Muriel Adams, Eva Love, -?-, -?-. Front row: Estella Hancox, Muriel Tromans, Mrs Rock, Winnie Jones, Ivy Tromans. Some of the children are Velma Willetts, Michael Hopkins, Susan Jones, Christopher Wright, Janet Mole and Robert Smith. *(Kath Mole)*

ACKNOWLEDGEMENTS

T hanks are expressed to all those individuals and organisations that have loaned pictures for this publication. These have been credited to the original photographer wherever possible, and failing that to the person loaning the picture. Permission to use copyright photographs has been sought where this has been known, and apologies are extended for inadvertent use of any material.

Once again special thanks must be extended to Jeff Jephcott, Editor (News Group) for the use of photographs and material from the *County Express*; the Black Country Living Museum (BCLM); the Black Country Society (BCS); The *Black Country Bugle*, Halesowen Library and Sandwell Community History and Archive Service (CHAS); and individually to Ken Rock for making his collection of postcards freely available.

The author intends to donate profits from the sale of this book to the Extension Fund of Hurst Green Methodist Church, and extends his thanks to all who will contribute to the appeal by purchasing this publication.